Silly Times with Two Silly Trolls

story by Nancy Jewell

pictures by Lisa Thiesing

■ HarperCollins*Publishers*

HarperCollins®, 👑®, and I Can Read™ are trademarks of HarperCollins Publishers Inc.

Silly Times with Two Silly Trolls
Text copyright © 1996 by Nancy Jewell
Illustrations copyright © 1996 by Lisa Thiesing
Printed in the U.S.A. All rights reserved.

Library of Congress Cataloging-in-Publication Data
Jewell, Nancy.
   Silly times with two silly trolls / story by Nancy Jewell ; pictures by Lisa
Thiesing.
      p.   cm. — (An I can read book)
   Summary: Two trolls, Nip and Tuck, discuss the difference between here
and there, write poems while sliding on the ice, and find an old clock that is
stopped at five o'clock.
   ISBN 0-06-024292-2. — ISBN 0-06-024293-0 (lib. bdg.)
   [1. Trolls—Fiction.]   I. Thiesing, Lisa, ill.   II. Title.   III. Series.
PZ7.S55325Si   1996   95-4319
[E]—dc20   CIP
                                                                      AC

1   2   3   4   5   6   7   8   9   10
❖
First Edition

For Trolls, Elves, and Fairies
Wherever you find them

—N. J.

For my daughter, Katherine

—L. T.

Contents

Here and There

"Come here, Tuck,"

said Nip.

"I am here," called Tuck

from the other room.

"You are not here," called Nip.

"I want you to come here."

Tuck looked at his hands.

He looked at his feet.

He patted his belly

and pinched his cheek.

"But I *am* here," called Tuck.

"No," called Nip,

"only I am here."

13

Tuck looked to his right.

He looked to his left.

He looked up and down
and all around.

"I don't see you,"
called Tuck.

"You can't see me," called Nip.

"Why?" called Tuck.

"Because you are not here

to see me," called Nip.

15

"Can you see me?" Tuck called.

"No," called Nip,

"because you are not here!"

"But where am I?" called Tuck.

16

"You are There," called Nip.

"Where is There?" called Tuck.

"There is not Here!" called Nip.

"But where is Here?" called Tuck.

"Here is where I am," called Nip.

17

"How do I get to Here?" called Tuck.

"You come to where I am," called Nip.

So Tuck walked into the room

where Nip was.

"Now I am here," Tuck said.

"Yes," said Nip.

"Now we are both here."

21

"Why did you want me here?"

said Tuck.

"I forget," said Nip.

22

Ice Is Nice

The trolls went for a walk.

"Ouch!" said Tuck.

"I bumped my head."

"Does it hurt?" asked Nip.

24

"No," said Tuck,

"but that bump made a lump."

"You made a poem," said Nip.

"Yes," said Tuck.

"Make another," said Nip.

Tuck thought and thought.

"Trees are green," he said.

"That was not a good poem," said Nip.

"It is hard to make a poem,"

said Tuck.

"Let me try," said Nip.

Nip thought and thought.

"I am stuck, Tuck," said Nip.

"I like that poem," said Tuck.

"What poem?" said Nip.

"I am stuck, Tuck," said Tuck.

The trolls came to an ice patch.

Nip took a step and fell down.

"You slipped, Nip," said Tuck.

Nip got up

and fell again.

"I slipped twice," he said.

"You slipped twice on the ice,"
said Tuck.

"It is nice to slip on the ice,"
said Nip.

"It is nice to slip twice
on the ice," said Tuck.

And the trolls slipped and slid,

and made poems about ice

for the rest of the day.

The Clock

One day the trolls

found an old clock.

"What time is it?" asked Nip.

"Five o'clock," said Tuck.

"Good," said Nip.

"It is time for supper."

"We already ate our supper,"

said Tuck.

"We will eat it again," said Nip.

The trolls ate supper again.

Then the trolls got ready for bed.

The clock still said five o'clock.

"Time moves slowly," said Nip.

"It moves very slowly," said Tuck.

The trolls went to sleep

and woke up with the sun.

"Our clock still says five,"

said Tuck.

"We will eat breakfast," said Nip.

"Maybe it will get later

after we eat."

The trolls ate breakfast

but the clock still said five.

They took a sunbath

and watered their flower.

They ate their lunch

and played a game of tag.

They ate a snack

and took a long nap.

The clock still said five.

The trolls ate supper

and took a walk until dark.

They brushed their teeth

and looked at their book.

Then they climbed into bed.

43

"Our clock still says

five o'clock," said Tuck.

"It said five o'clock all day,"

said Nip.

"And all last night," said Tuck.

44

"Time is funny," said Nip.

"Yes," said Tuck.

"It is always five o'clock."

The trolls said good night

and turned out the light.

In the morning

they checked the clock.

"It still says five o'clock,"

said Tuck.

"Good," said Nip.

"Our clock is on time."